MW00909233

# Nice Try, Katrina!

## Trials of a Hurricane Katrina Evacuee

**Kendra Marie Harris**

Copyright © 2006 by Kendra Marie Harris

ISBN 0-7414-3323-0

*Published by:*

PUBLISHING.COM

*1094 New DeHaven Street, Suite 100*
*West Conshohocken, PA 19428-2713*
*Info@buybooksontheweb.com*
*www.buybooksontheweb.com*
*Toll-free (877) BUY BOOK*
*Local Phone (610) 941-9999*
*Fax (610) 941-9959*

*Printed in the United States of America*

*Printed on Recycled Paper*

*Published July 2006*

*Story dedicated to my grandparents and their eldest daughter.*

*Also, my devotion is with my dearest sister-friend, Shelley Patrice Baham*

Enduring the hardship of life
Sustaining the blows of the storm
Tuning to the silent messages with a special kind
of listening only given by God
Sheltering the wilderness - light through a dark
path - self-indulgence ever so does repeat
but His grace guides my feet

Swallowed up by worldly sharks
Taunted by the whispers which lark
my every dream with desires to mark
To lean on faith - biting the devil's bate
Mirages living, the mind a thresh
Walking in this cruel world fooled by the tainted
tasty evils of refresh
But one drop, only one to remain in an array of
dispense - letting the asphalt take away dignity
and confidence
When the battle is fought and the raging of the
storm is calm
When the homeless is hovered and the bare
covered
When the golden narrow path becomes grazed
with your prints and dents and sideward bends
When you've been good in spite of and loved
those enemies called friends
When your armor is weather beaten and the
victory is won
REJOICE! REJOICE!
For the Father says "Servant Well Done!"

## The Gumbo Bowl

It was August, the hottest month in New Orleans. But instead of enjoying this hot summer month's end, I was making a decision that would soon change my life. August 28, 2005 fell on a Sunday. I was unable to sleep for worry of the hurricane that would soon destroy my home.

After convincing those family members and friends to leave the city prior to Hurricane Katrina (I was on the phone 5:30 in the morning calling and warning), we were on the road. Packed with G.G, Mama, and Valentin, my Cavalier was going on a journey. Before the start of this journey, my brother, who was threatened into following me out of the city and transporting Tia and Trey, had to make a stop. It was to the house of his girlfriend who was riding in his car too. Love had to, at least, make sure Fam was secured and had something to eat. There was no room for him in either car. And we were off. We thought! Time had zoomed by.

It took four hours of convincing and negotiating to get these people to pack something and leave. My convincing turned to screaming, crying, cussing and damn near fighting but I knew their plan to go to the Superdome would not work out. It was a gut feeling. Time was still passing, and I was shaken. I had to get over the number of times I called to learn of my mother's evacuation plan. We, Valentin, my children and I, stopped over before heading out to the highway. This is when I became a little emotional because I could not believe that they had not done anything in preparation for this evacuation. My brother was asleep on the floor in the living room and his girlfriend asleep on the sofa. My mother was sitting on her bed with the news station broadcasting – telling her to leave. My grandmother was sitting at the kitchen table unable to really get around and draining liquid from her back. Oh My God! I lost my mind. It's amazing what happens when you get a little crazy. "What are y'all doing?" My mother answered, "We're going to the Superdome if anything really happens." "Mama, New Orleans has never had a category 5 hurricane and I don't think the Superdome will be safe." Well, after begging and pleading, and crying, she started to put a few clothes in a bag. But my brother did not move. He was set on going to the Superdome. I was driving an old Cavalier and my two children, my boyfriend, my mother, my grandmother and our belongings could not all travel in that car. After all, I had to find room for my mother's dialysis machine. She has to dialyze every night. Ugly words were shouted and feelings were hurt and, at last, my brother got up.

So now here we were, gridlocked! We were on Airline Highway for hours and going no where. Oh! I was stressed but working to calm down but emotional still because of all I went through to get these people to leave New Orleans. Cars were breaking down in the turtling traffic. Families were cramped into the back of pick ups. We were out of gas! We stopped to get gas and got back into traffic, seemingly, in the same spot we were before pulling into a gas station. "1 – 2 – 3," I have heard that counting gives enough time to mentally sustain. Everyone in the car, at this time, was antsy. Boogie, my brother, and I began entertaining one another as we drove. He would call me on my cell phone and tell jokes and I, in turn, would call him to make sure he was awake.

The time had come once again, hours later, to refill the cars with gas. We seemed to be in the middle of nowhere. It was black as the back of shut eyelids. Car lights were the only form of illumination for a long stretch of the road. I called 911. "I am evacuating, I am running out of gas, I cannot see anything, please help me?!" All of this poured from my mouth as I became nervous. Becoming stranded, I thought to my self, would be the ultimate obstacle. "What do you see around you?" Didn't I just tell this woman that I could not see a thing, I thought as I answered her. "M'am, I see nothing but a row of car lights behind me through the rear view mirror and red brake lights from the cars ahead of me as we inch along. There are trees and road." I held the line until some sort of landmark was visible. The operator then led me to a gas station off of the main highway. It was easy to locate because it was the only source of light in that area. But Godda…! The line of cars to enter was extremely long. It was out of the station, two blocks down the road and continuing to lengthen. The only way for me to remain in this present day, and not flip out as I would have back in the day, was to think of my newly discovered spiritual strength. It is newly discovered only because over recent years I have tapped into what has always been there. My life has been so unbalanced and I, as a result, was a time bomb (to be nice when giving a description about myself). I believe it started with the death of my father and the surgery to remove the brain tumor with which I was born. This happened in the same year within a few months of each other, it seemed. The operation came first. I remember my daddy holding my hand and rubbing my head. I felt him and smelled him. But I was unconscious. I will never forget. Who I also remember is my aunt, my mother's sister. I saw her when I was being transported to the operating room. Heavily sedated, I saw her. Auntie Cheryl always spoke up on my behalf. She was hailing assistance because someone left me out in the hallway at Charity Hospital. Although, Charity was a very good hospital – the best some might say; it wasn't the safest place (my family thought). Charity was a vacation home for the homeless schizophrenics and drug addicts. It was a familiar scene for the thugs and innocents that were stabbed, shot or beaten bloody. It was the place that accepted unwed young mothers without insurance, like my mama, to give birth. I was born there as was the majority of black New Orleans. But Charity housed the best doctors.

They were teaching doctors and medical students from LSU and Tulane. For this reason, people, both white and black, traveled many miles to be treated. In most instances, Charity Hospital was all there was for the middle class and below. Dr. Ennis was the head surgeon when I was there. The tumor was successfully removed but my mother was told I would not be able to achieve highly. I would be average or below. I had lost all function in the right side of my body. So, I guess, this seemed to be true to her. But I have been carried by the ancestors and protected by God. They told me I will never live according to someone else's limitations. My grandfather taught me to write again. He gave me inspiration. But I struggled. Struggled to over stand the obstacles I had been faced with that were no fault of my own. It was just the hand I was dealt. I struggled. I began writing poetry. It was therapy. Therapy allowed me to deal with the fact that my mother accepted me as handicapped and I just didn't fit in with the rest of the children at Joseph A. Craig Elementary School. I had become a much older soul or I had been equipped with the "Souls of Black Folk" (W.E.B. Dubois). They filled my cavity of a body like a hollow tooth. It seemed to me that they lived in Treme, the souls of the ancestors. I was taught that dope is death in Treme. I was taught the significance of Congo Square where slaves bartered commodities and held reunions on Sundays in Treme. I was taught to open up just a little at my elementary school which was located in the heart of Treme, the oldest neighborhood in the country for free blacks. This neighborhood encompassed St. Augustine Catholic Church, a church founded by slaves. But I had also developed hatred for men in Treme, where my mother lived with her husband after moving out of the Iberville Housing Project. He beat me! I was angry. I fought boys (and girls) at school and in church. I did not talk to any man who spoke to me. That anger shifted by some means when I surprising became popular in junior high school and throughout high school. I was still reckless. There were many prices to pay.

G.G. rode shot gun. My grandmother, G.G., had just dressed herself and called for a ride from the hospital on the Friday before the hurricane and there was no way she was going to the Superdome, just now diagnosed with Cancer, as long as I had breath in my body. She was ready though. "Ma big granbaby gon take car'o me." "Let's ride," she said.

Back on that journey, on Airline Highway, we inched and stopped, and inched and stopped, and inched and he hit me, my brother, with his car. He hit me so hard I hit the truck in front of me. He fell asleep. Strength and patience is what I asked for at that time, guidance from my ancestors. "What would the ancestors do?" I remained calm in appearance and got out of the car. The driver of the small pick up got out of the truck too! People were yelling, "Move off of the road!" while blowing their horns and shouting obscenities. "Lord, help me?" My brother did not even get out. In fact, he began yelling at me to get back in the car and "c'mon!," he said. "Nothing is wrong with that truck!" "Man, we ain't got time for that!" I got in my car and drove away, in pain. I swear, with all the pinned up stress I carried, if it wasn't for the look on my grandmother's face that said we are still family, it would have been a beating on Airline. But we made it to Baton Rouge finally. I needed to get to a hospital. G.G.'s catheter, which was placed in her back to help drain the toxins because the tumor was too large to allow them to drain from her bladder, leaked. It leaked and bled on her clothes, in the car, and on her spirit. It leaked. But they were proud – "We'll make it!" "I don't want to go to no hospital." That was my mama, strapped with a catheter herself and in need to be dialyzed. I pulled up to the General Hospital and they were reluctant to take them but "no" was not setting too well with me then. They were placed, together, in a triage room, both refusing to see a doctor. I left with Valentin and my children. Boogie left too. Without us there they would have no choice but to cooperate with the staff. Boogie and Love slept in the parking lot of the hospital and we rode a couple of miles back to the Waffle House. After eating, we slept in the parking lot across the street at the strip mall. The winds from Hurricane Katrina woke us. Signs fells, poles crashed, and the electric wires slammed together causing fire and sparks that terrified my children. Hell, it scared me too! But there we were, at least we weren't in New Orleans.

The winds tamed themselves just enough for me to gain the courage to drive back to the hospital. Boogie and Love were still in the car, afraid to get out. Together, we went into the hospital expecting to have a whole heap of anger thrown at us. My mama and G.G. was right where we left them, in the triage room. My mama explained the staff that had come on for the new day was very nasty. The head nurse told them to leave because no one had authorization to accept them. This was my argument: Too late! The overnight staff had already given my grandmother a place to clean up and my mother a place to dialyze. Were they going to put them out on the street? They both had insurance. Was it their fault they weren't given a room or even seen by a doctor? The paperwork was complete for admitting. I did it myself before leaving the previous night. Although, they were hesitant to see a doctor, they knew it was best. It would have been wise. Come to find out, these people never even stuck their head in the room or knocked. And the paperwork, I went to the desk to learn had been shuffled around until they were no longer visible to the intake processors. We were not their usual patients, I found after looking around. The only people with faces like mine were the maintenance and kitchen employees. This gave me more fuel. It wasn't fuel to become irate but fuel to show that I am a child of Africans tainted by the New World, child

8

of Congo Square with pride given by the slaves who danced there on Sundays. I am blessed by the ancestors and I walk that way.

We remained without a place to go. I attempted once again to have Mama and G.G. stay at the hospital another night but this time they weren't having it at all. I went to the playroom with my four year old son, Trey. We spent a little time there, in the hospital. We visited the cafeteria and even took a little nap in the playroom that was three rooms made into one because now there were more people without a place to go coming into the hospital. Later, we were up and ready to go. Mama and G.G. were packed, dressed and at the door for the journey to continue. "We ain't staying here no more." But I explained to G.G. that we were sleeping in the car or on the ground and I just didn't think she should be exposed to those circumstances. She wasn't hearing it. My mother just stood and looked at me with the same look that frightened me as a child – I am still her little girl and that look – so we all were in the car. I drove with no direction after the rain and wind stopped beating the tree limbs and buildings of the hospital. It was almost dark and the question had come again, "Where do we sleep?" Well, I tried calling a distant cousin who leaves in Baton Rouge but her number had been changed and was not listed. I tried calling one of my mother's co-workers from Southern University at New Orleans who lived in Baton Rouge but the answering machine picked up and I never received a call back. I tried the local shelters but they were all full. So I tried another parking lot. This one was to an outpatient care facility operated by LSU. We parked toward the back corner of the private lot near the dumpster for fear that we would be told to vacate. I was tired. My brother had abandoned us. He drove to Alexandria by Love's family where there were 18 people in and out of a one bedroom apartment. So in the parking lot were Tia, Trey, Valentin, G.G., Mama, and me, of course. The children slept in front seat. My mama and G.G. slept in the back seat. Valentin and I slept on a blanket behind the car. I always carried blankets in the car because when time permitted I would go to City Park. I loved it there. That was my beautiful. There should always be a place in your heart, a place you can go to and find a beautiful mental relaxation haven. City Park was my beautiful.

There we were, asleep. Valentin said I even snored as loud as lions roared –I was tired. The morning came; it was time to get on the road again. I did not want the employees of this facility to report to work and find a family slumbering on the grounds. The people of Baton Rouge didn't seem to understand, in my opinion. There were jobs for them to report to, we didn't even have homes, never mind employment. I knew the levees were broken back home because it was all that was on the radio but I could not explain that to my grandmother. I turned the radio off whenever she was around. She wanted to go home. "G.G. we can't go home, they're not letting us go home because the water has covered the city." "What water chile," she asked without a clue of the disaster that had wiped us out. G.G.'s house was in the hardest hit area, the Lower Ninth Ward. Her house, that she shared with my grandfather, who had died two months before the hurricane, was one block from the Industrial Canal. Pawpaw was a carpenter. He built most of the interior for the neighborhood pre-school and the neighbor's homes. I remember when I was a little girl, Pawpaw and I walked up and down Deslonde St. visiting people. He would talk about jazz, and the war in which he fought, and black history. He told us what it was like when blacks didn't have much. But he taught me to be proud and determined. He said that's how he made it. He also built my aspirations to acquire an education. He was one known for his penmanship, after all he had taught himself to read and write. Pawpaw didn't get very much from his five years in elementary school. He had to help his grand-mother raise his brother and sisters (I don't know what happened to Mariah, his mother, and I don't know anything about his father). But don't reckon with him, he was a very intelligent military man and self-sufficient black father. He was married for fifty-nine years before he died. Everyone loved him. "G.G., we can't go home," this was all I could say.

*And it happened early that Monday morning,*
*Blowing over the land of the Gulf Coast*
*Striking the flood gates at the levees*
*The Olde Creole Queen, as we know her, was*
*striped of her gut*
*You took from her*
*the forever growing cultured souls*
*refined with all the Cajun spices that*
*seasoned her land*
*But she wants it back, the gut of her existence*
*She wants them back, the culture bearers*
*from the beginning of her time*
*The descendants of Bienville, Jeff Davis,*
*Napoleon, the city sublime*
*The descendants of the Thibodaux,*
*Boudreauxs and Rouselles*
*playing jazz in ragtime*
*She wants them back*
*The descendants of the Bambara, Mandinka,*
*Fulani, Wolof*
*and all other souls that sizzled holding the*
*blistering torch*
*as their psychological beings were attacked*
*She wants them back*
*The descendants of the ones who leaped in the*
*air dancing on free market Sunday at Congo*
*Square,*
*She wants them back*
*I am frail, she said, trembling and bleeding*
*and soaked from the muddy waters that filled*
*this bowl on that day*
*I am squealing, weeping and still hissing at*
*the memories of my cultured souls being*
*washed away*

*I am searching, hoping, and calling for the
ones who are gone astray
I am sending peace to the ones who were
troubled without love and
leaning to a life of crime and dismay
I am shining immense lighting for those who
have lost there way
But pray, pray souls, to the African Powers
For they have the ultimate power
Reach up and get the power
Reach forward and receive the power
Reach back and give the power
Reach down, gain ancestral power
They've walked here before
Come back, my souls, run no more
Stand forcefully, run no more*

14

We continued to drive. I became lost and what seemed to be a curse was actually a blessing. Using physical vision, the flat tire the car sat on as we sat on a dirt road with, deceptively, no end was the extreme obstacle to cross over, I thought to myself. No one but Valentin saw that I was totally discouraged. He hugged me and said it's alright. He had me to see where I had carried my family, out of harms way and he reassured me that it would be just a matter of time before I find a place for G.G. and Mama. He was right. Valentin put the doughnut spare on the car. We looked for a place to buy a tire, a used tire. We didn't have much money.

Before we left New Orleans, Valentin had just come to my house from Shreveport, where he worked, to be with my children and me at the time of a potential disaster. He came back with a check to cash but everything was closed. We had a few dollars for gas to get on the road to some place near. He was skeptical of the severity of the storm that was headed toward us. But I was alone with Tia and Trey, so he felt he should be with us. Valentin and I were preparing to deal with immigration before Katrina. He is from Honduras. But we had been together for six months and he was really assuming the responsibility which was dropped by my ex-husband. I loved him for that. I stopped at a gas station to ask the location of the nearest tire shop. The cashier, who appeared to be amazed at how different my dialect was from hers (New Orleans drawl, I guess), pointed me in the direction of a shop down the street. Here, the man tried persistently to sell me a new tire. I explained to him that we were from New Orleans and we haven't much money and no place to go. He went beyond his duty for us. "Oh, I have sixteen people in my home from New Orleans right now and I know it can't be easy for you all out here." He said, "I don't have a used tire to fit your car but I have one just a little smaller than the size on your car. We are going to rotate your tires and put the smaller one on the back at no charge – you should be alright." This man went into his shop and had an employee call hotels around Zachary, LA to find shelter for my family. I didn't even know we had driven so far that we were in another city. There were no hotel rooms available. The employee called his church. This was the blessing. Their church was preparing a shelter for those who had been displaced and wandering, like us. We went there. I felt a ton of pressure taking flight off of my shoulders because my mama and G.G. had a safe place to stay. But there was one problem – Mama's dialysis machine was in the trunk of my brother's car and he was in Alexandria. All the pressure was thrown back on me, which is the way I felt anyway. "Bruce, can you bring Mama's machine to Zachary?" "I don't know, I'ma see," is what he told me. I was furious. "Who told your ass to leave us anyway? You know our stuff is in your car!" My brother, my mama's baby, never came. The church arranged for her to go to a hospital in Baton Rouge to learn to dialyze herself manually. They transported her and paid for the service. We were comforted. We also knew we could not stay here too long. We only had two weeks.

Boogie and Love arrived in Zachary, eventually. He stayed overnight to see G.G. (Queen G.G. is what they called her at the shelter). He slept on the floor next to her. Boogie never really displayed sentimental emotion in his life but to know him is to know when he is hurting. He stays away when he is hurting. He is the youngest grandchild of all of the grand-children. The next day they went back to Alexandria. But the time had come for us to move on.

On the way to Texas, I met Boogie on the highway. We were off once again. We drove to Farmers Branch, Texas. G.G.'s sisters were there. They had evacuated to my cousin's two bedroom apartment. When we arrived, there were 20 people, including us. One of my cousins rented an apartment in the same complex so that is where Valentin and I slept. I learned that FEMA provided hotel rooms to evacuees. We went to the nearest hotel to apply. It was the Crowne Plaza on Midway Road in Addison, Texas. We were relieved. Later, I drove my mother to get a room. Silently, I hoped it wasn't near my room. I was exhausted and needed space. The rooms were next door to each other. Still later, we went back to get my brother, whose room was across the hall. For our stay though, he managed to vanish even when he was in the hotel. His father showed up at the hotel after being released from a Mississippi jail on a misdemeanor charge from many years ago that should have been cleared. We hadn't seen him in awhile. But we, including me, were all glad to see him in Texas. Valentin and I tried to remain high spirited even though we had lost everything (his clothes were there too). Without even seeing my house we knew there was no hope because the house was three blocks on the other side of the Industrial Canal, in the Upper Ninth Ward. The only thing we were not certain of is whether or not the house was standing. We heard of houses collapsing and people drowning on the radio. "What are we going to do?" I found an apartment in Addison, after being turned down twice because of my credit score. What a time to refuse a place to accommodate those displaced by rickety levees. My credit has been ruined due to my expired marriage. My ex-husband failed to pay the car note for a car we owned jointly on paper but was his exclusively. The car was repossessed. I also moved from the apartment we shared without timely notification. That's what they said! But I gave written notice and paid the rent on time while I resided in Georgetown Apartment Homes. I had money and I was educated. I paid a mortgage in New Orleans. But I was asked, even with the information on the application, if my prior governmental housing assistance and welfare were active. What the $&%*? It seems that everyone outside of New Orleans has the impression that the residents of my city are poor, ignorant bastards. We were talked to as if we were idiots. Everyone I spoke with complained of the same. Racial inequalities were soaring through the air of the south. The discrimination that lived dormant was washed up and exposed as Katrina saturated southern soil. The true definition of the American Way was bare.

*Look at me*
*Not with just your eyes*
*See the inner me, deep down within me*
*Know who I am, not who I could be*
*Listen to me*
*Not with just your ears*

*Hear the sound I make so dear*
*Hear my laugh, my cry, my scream of fear*
*Know the sound that comes from me,*
*not what should be*
*Touch me*
*Not with just your hands*
*Feel my heart beat*
*Know where I stand*
*Feel my joy, feel that I am human*
*Know that I am different in the sun and the*
*rain*
*Know that crying and sighing, loving and*
*laughing I can*
*Smell me*
*Not with just a sniff*
*Know that my scent can be pleasant or it can*
*be stiff*
*Know that my scent can last forever or it can*
*breeze through swift*
*Know my natural scent comes from me - only*
*me*
*Taste me*
*Not with just a your buds*
*Feel the sensation, the bitter floods*
*See I am different just with a lick so be careful*
*of the flavor you pick*
*Know me*
*As me*
*For me*
*Accept me*
*Love me*
*Know I am me*
*Not who I could be*
*Not who I should be*

*To know me is to*
*See me*
*To listen to me*
*To feel me*
*To smell me*
*To taste me*
*Before you judge me*
*First, I ask that you simply know me*


We lived in a two bedroom apartment. Amina and her mama shared an apartment with the same floor plan as ours. We inhaled, and then exhaled for relief. G.G. lived no where but New Orleans in all of her seventy-eight years. She liked the apartment. An apartment that, was just an apartment to me, was elaborate to my grandmother. She was becoming very ill but still refusing treatment. I watched her. She was dying. But she was happy in that apartment. We laughed and danced and basically carried on as if we were down in New Orleans. It was the way for us. "Forget your sorrow and dance. Forget your trouble and dance," Bob Marley said that. Auntie Cheryl visited us for Thanksgiving. She was there, also to see her mama and help my mama take care her. She came from Plaquemine, LA. The evacuation led her there. Oh! I was happy to see her. She is my favorite aunt. She is my Big Momma. I loved her so. We played cards – she was the one who taught me to play Spades at age 9 and had been my partner ever since. We talked, ate, and laughed. Soon it was time for her to leave. "I'll be back for Christmas and I want one of them!" She was talking about a wooden incense box with picturesque motifs carved into the wood. I had begun to make jewelry and sell oils, African art and artifacts in Texas while I sat bored to tears. I searched for employment, and although qualified, over qualified for some positions, I was not employed because I was from New Orleans. Employers often thought of the possibilities of New Orleans residents returning home and others just flat out refuse to hire. She wanted an incense box.

Auntie Cheryl never made it back to Texas. She was getting dressed one evening in Plaquemine to go to the Casino with her new friends. She was going to the Casino with her friends that had provided her a place to live. These were friends that were, in number years, older than her but called her Ms. Cheryl for her wisdom. She died. She had a stroke/aneurysm. The doctors said she became brain died in a short period of time. It drove me crazy not to be able to get to her. She was always there for me. Two weeks before Christmas, my family went to New Orleans to bury her. My cousins, Auntie Cheryl's children, could not be alone at this time. How are they going to accept their mother's death? Pressure had weighed in on everybody. Back in Texas, G.G. had a seizure. My mother was afraid to tell me - but my grandmother had a seizure. We could not take her to New Orleans because she had become so weak. She had a seizure provoked by anxiety while we were gone.

The day before my thirtieth birthday my mama had a series of seizures. She had a stroke and a succession of seizures. The doctors told me to call my family because she was not going to make it. I am trying to forget the pain from those memories of mama in a coma and just one year later, G.G. had a seizure. "I can't do this! I can't take no more!" But life assured me that we all have to endure to come out on the brighter side. And besides, I needed to be strong for my mother. She had just lost her father and sister. She is now losing her mother.

Well, G.G. passed away two days into the New Year. She came with us into the year 2006. Two weeks after burying my aunt, my family and I went back to New Orleans to bury my grandmother. I really can't take it no more.

Tia and Trey attend Holy Ghost Catholic School in New Orleans. They have never attended a catholic school before. I have never paid tuition for my daughter to go to school. She attended a chartered school before the hurricane. The International School of Louisiana prepared her for our Texas experience. We were in a Hispanic community. With her Spanish curriculum, she knew how to communicate effectively. It even came in handy for me at times when I needed to communicate with someone that spoke too fast for me to understand. It came in handy when she had to say goodbye to her friends because we were going back to New Orleans. I couldn't take any more of being away from my home.

We, my children, Valentin and I, live in the Marriott Hotel now. I am in graduate school at Southern University @ New Orleans. The flame that ensue my determination to complete my studies must never dwindle. I will succeed because I refuse to limit myself. Earning a doctorate degree has been a goal that I will accomplish for myself and for Shelley Patrice Baham. For as long as I can remember, Shelley was my very best friend in the world; she died of cancer in November 2002. I became numb. I began thinking that I had lost the only person in the world that understood me and still genuinely loved me.

*Are you the soul who calls out for companionship?*
*Are you the one who watches the sparkle of the stars at night?*
*(the one that implore some form of salvation)*
*I know you, companionless one, the lonely soul without a friend*
*Your life is filled with many doleful moments, your days - melancholy actions,*
*never having anything of significance to do*
*I know what you stand for*
*You're so lonely and so confused*
*Why are you so mysterious, such a nebbish being?*
*Why are you so full of anxiety?*
*You see in the mirror a nobody who's going nowhere so why try?*
*Nobody understands you, nobody except me*
*I'm just like you*

We were to go back to school together but her dreams were cut short so they will live through my accomplishments. I will succeed for her. Also at present, I am trying to figure out the best way to rebuild my house which was completely destroyed due to Hurricane Katrina – they say. Now that my mortgage is paid, I have accomplished one of my goals. That goal is holding ownership of my home, escaping the burdensome cloud that hangs over ones head when lien holders are involved. It was a blessing from God delivered by Katrina. Although the insurance companies have been close to invisible, I know, somehow, I will figure out a way to repair my home. We will succeed. But many times I feel like <u>we're</u> alone – apart from the United States Government. Yes, New Orleans is rebuilding but not really in my neighborhood. We are trying to get things together ourselves aside from the assistance provided by FEMA for rental assistance or the FEMA "shut up, you nuisance" money. I was taught to survive. This is a story bearing similarities to most people's strife and victories that occur in their lives when dealing with pain, losses and determination. There are few people to share the heartbreaking details outside of therapy sessions or support groups. My grandfather told me that clear expression comes through writing. The name Karasi Monet Brumfield carries a legacy given by Walter Brumfield, Sr. I will succeed because it never occurs to me to do otherwise. Pawpaw taught me that.

*It was long ago...*
*I have almost forgotten my dream*
*But it was there, then, in front of me,*
*Bright like the sun*
*And then a wall 'rose, 'rose slowly*
*Between me and my dream*
*'Rose slowly*
*Dimming, hiding the light of my dream*
*'Rose slowly,*
*Until it touched the sky-*
*The wall shadowed me*
*I lie in the shadow —*
*no longer the light before me*
*Above me*
*Only the thick wall, the shadow*
*My hands! My dark hands!*
*Break through the wall*
*Find my dream*
*Shatter this deathlike dusk*
*Break this shadow into a thousand rays of*
*sunbeams*
*To illuminate my dream*

**Trey Bostich**

*Father said, there were leaders who gave up*
*life for the cause –*
*people to stand all wars*
*But they stopped breathing*
*"Keep thy heart with all diligence; for out of it*
*are the issues of life"*
*But without it what makes life for me*
*I hear tranquil breezes, yet murmured clatter*
*and I feel your withdrawal, mama*
*Father said, I am his and you are never to*
*misguide me*
*but already I am experiencing growing pains,*
*seeing stains of evil through your skin*
*Been swallowing poisons as every sound wave*
*hits your eardrum*
*From this confusion, mama, I ask, what's*
*going on?*
*I feel your touch which teaches the*
*importance of libation*
*and smile at your soothing*
*lullabies by wise men*
*and it makes me know love is there*
*But I know not where, mama*
*I hear about manifest destiny and with*
*Father, I have met the Freedom*
*Riders and Oretha Haley*
*I listened to Biko tell of apartheid, listened to*
*Mr. King tell of the stride*

*to the statue of Lincoln while drinking*
*impressionable juice*
*Choking when I saw the horrendous scars of*
*hatred on Emmit's face*
*The fast paced beat of my heart scares me*
*But Mother Tubman cuddles me and says it's*
*alright black child*
*for we have made a way*
*Now I am almost here and Father whispers in*
*my ear –*
*"No weapon formed against you shall*
*prosper"*
*But there are no leaders just "up until the*
*battle" marchers*
*because the die hard leaders have stopped*
*breathing*
*What am I to do – There's not even an*
*education advocacy –*
*remembering Mrs. Bethune's Institute and*
*Mrs. Lucy Foster's longevity*
*What will I become?*
*Father said, "A powerful leader in my name,*
*son, until the day you stop breathing!"*


My mommy woke me up extra early, I think. She tiptoed pass my door like she always does; she was trying not to wake me but it doesn't matter. I get up when she goes by. I saw her walking with clothes in her arms and mumbling to herself. When she's like this I know it's something grave happening or going to happen. The last time she mumbled to herself, my daddy had married another woman and I thought she was going to kill him. She thought she was going to kill him. My daddy lived in our house. We were a family. They were back together to mend the family that already existed in my eyes. He moved back in and they looked happy. I know Mommy was happy because she felt there was space left to proceed with the family she cherished so dearly. She wanted to forget the day she threatened Daddy if he didn't sign the divorce papers. My daddy would play with us, me and my sister. And we were happy too. But he married another woman and we didn't know. Daddy had two lives for a while…well until my mommy found out. My mommy also found out that he was sleeping around with other women. I don't exactly know what that means but I know my daddy should have only gone nite-nite with my mommy because he was in trouble.

Before I was born, my mommy said her life had become filled with purpose. She and my sister had gotten married to my daddy. Daddy asked her for a son and my mommy said she hesitated to oblige because my sister's father had hurt her. She said she was afraid to become a mommy again. But she loved daddy and took full position as his wife. She thought, "My husband has asked for a child and I will please him." I was born in November of 2001. Mommy had become very ill toward the end of her pregnancy. She said I was too heavy for her pelvic bone – whatever that is. But finally the time had come. I was a healthy baby boy weighing 8 pounds and

2 ounces. She was happy and sad. She was sad, because I was born blue and purple. I had swallowed blood and could not breathe when I came down the birth canal. I don't think I was ready the first time down so I traveled back. Mommy couldn't talk. She said she was in too much pain to inform the nurse, who was about two feet away. She and the doctor were watching the night time sitcoms on the delivery room's television set. In her mind, though, she yelled repetitively and very loudly, "My baby is coming!!!!" But I fought to stay in this world, remembering the soothing touch through mommy's skin and her muttered melodic voice as she whispered African proverbs. I would listen to her tell me things like "It is easy to defeat people who do not kindle the fire for themselves" or "If God breaks your leg He will teach you how to limp so always have faith that you will endure, young King." I believed every word.

My parents argued all of the time about my daddy never being home. He worked offshore and stayed at work months at a time. When he came home, he went by his friends. My mommy would scream bad words at him. She started to believe my daddy had a problem with her because she was American and he was Honduran. Sometimes daddy would hug her as she cried holding me in her arms. He told her that those things she believed to be true were not. She wanted to know the reason he drank so much, after all she worked hard to be the best wife she could be for him. But mommy was there before he started working offshore. She said she didn't really know my daddy anymore. My daddy had his own demons. He also had many obstacles in his life that he allowed to block his path so he remained in one place. Mommy just couldn't make him face the obstacles or the demons. Because he stayed away on the water for so long, mommy began to accept the untruth of her being single. She dated other men. There was a man who would come to see her but he only visited us for short periods of time. Mommy said he made her feel special. He bought flowers for her and toys for me and my sister. He even brought breakfast, lunch and/or dinner when mommy didn't move from the bed because she was so sad. Mommy said he was a virtuous friend but in her heart she realized the likeliness of her accepting another man's love. To her, at that time, her marriage had failed so she divorced my daddy.

*Tall, deep chocolate brown skin, bald, large*
*hands, strong, muscular build, wise, gentle*
*man – I fell in love with him*
*He is my love – never made music; I didn't*
*want to accept love until one year…*
*Sweaty passion*
*Sticky love muscles*
*Soft tongue caresses sang crescendo tones*
*After the long time winds had blown I*
*wondered what did I do -*

*I really did love him. I praised his magisterial
presence.*
*I longed for the wisdom words that dripped
from his tongue*
*as we mentally sat on the shores of the Niger
River Delta*
*and listened to the ancestors sing*
*My skin dampened at his every minuscule
touch*
*but the time held too much*
*when he revealed his secret*
*Time held too much when I, too had the same
new secret*
*Two men – I loved them both- for different
reasons*
*and if combining them was an option, I
would have the perfect husband*
*but what about him – will his wife
understand this extended relationship*
*on the outer surface of matrimony –*
*that lady's husband forever lingers around
me*
*That lady's husband –*
*Tall, deep chocolate brown skin, bald, large
hands, strong, muscular*
*build, wise, gentle man –*
*I fell in love with him*
*He is my love*
*Twilight night shade of skin, broad shoulders,
locked lengthy hair, rough*
*man's man, beautiful spirited man –*
*I fell in love with him because...*
*He was my foundation, my support, my King
that cherished my soul*

*I felt his warm cares. I seized his*
*nourishment.*
*I tasted his love in the core of my being.*
*I am safe. And time held too much when I*
*married him.*


Tara lived in New York. Nelson was introduced to her by one of his friends. He drove to New York one evening after dropping me and my sister off at my mommy's job. He told my mommy he would be home after the weekend was over. He said that he was going to Texas with his friends to look for a truck to purchase. Tara was Honduran and Nelson Bostich, my daddy, didn't know her from their home country but she was from the same village. She was younger than my mommy. Mommy always called her "lil girl." But that was the next year when daddy got in trouble. Daddy was in trouble when my mommy found out that he had married Tara in New York. He married her after he was stabbed in the abdomen believing it was my mommy's fault. He was stabbed by a man in a Latin club who had danced with Mommy. Mommy said he always asked her to dance, that man. I think he liked her but my mommy just liked to dance and he was a good dancer. My daddy didn't want any man around my mommy. He would often fight with men that attempted to court her. All of the men who stood and admired Mommy in those Latin clubs were apprehensive to dance with her for that reason so she danced alone most of the time. She never cared. She said she danced to cleanse her soul. The sweat that trickled from her brow was little bulbs of negative energy being expelled from her sanguine spirit. But my daddy was jealous of any man who could possibly take away from him the person who loved him the most in his entire life. He stalked her! He even burglarized our home. It was Mommy's thirtieth birthday. She had some friends from out of town over to celebrate her years on earth. Nelson was told that they went out to a club and that Mommy was with one man in particular. This was amusing to my mommy being that she hadn't seen him for four days – he never even called to wish her a happy birthday. But he shattered the window to her bedroom early Sunday morning to drag one of Mommy's house guests out of the house on his back. Mommy fought to move from that place in her life that held her in mental bondage. She had to permit her heart love again but I, a growing baby boy, required a father.

*Keep your head to the sky*
*Is what I hear*
*Just leave me be with the mirrored reality*
*staring in my face*
*Sqreaching-chanting, I wish it was over, I*
*wish it was over - is my soul,*
*the voice of my spirit*
*is the hidden reality*

*Just leave me alone by myself to awake what
is real
to release the dark chains – boomerangs of
depression
to sleep and find fantasy because I've never
been happy
Just leave me a loan to buy the room furniture
for livin',
the kitchen eating table,
the food to nourish and call this home just
leave me alone
My friends, so-called friends, family, enemies
feeding off of my character
'cause you say I'm strong
because you're like thorns in my fingers,
splinters in my nose –
blood of the innocent on the hanging tree
you make me flee from your vibes because
dodging every blow is what
you see but you don't see me bleeding to
death*

*Keep your head to the sky
Just leave me a man, a masculine man, a
daddy, my daughter's daddy,
my son's daddy- to love and nurture their
seed
…to protect their own
I wish it was over so life could just leave me
alone*

<u>So I Dance</u>

*To find my soul*
*To feel a pulse*
*To live the music of the conga*
*I hear it - it talks to me - it tells me my destiny*
*To taste, drip by drip, on my tongue*
*The sauce of the drum*
*The words so righteous, the ancestors just*
*move me*
*So I dance*
*To heal all wounds*
*To soothe the scars in my womb*
*To conjure up praise for hours - never cease -*
*it tells my story of peace*
*I sing to harmonize with the harmony the*
*strings give*
*To deal with the scantiness of union*
*it ruins my diamonds that sparkle*
*To forgo hatred*
*The musico tells me to live for me*
*and the symphony explodes with tunes only I*
*hear*
*So I dance*
*To move  -  TO GET UP AND MOVE*
*To get up and move from worldly tracks*
*where X seems to MARK THE SPOT PUT*
*ASIDE FOR MY LIFE*
*Watching a train with blooded brakes coming*
*to take away my LIVELY self*
*But I'm standing on the tracks mentally*
*dancing*
*but paralyzed, blind, deaf*

*Standing on the tracks, STILL, standing,*
*dancing on the tracks*
*BEAT THE CONGA, STROKE THE STRINGS,*
*SING ME A SONG*
*To move me - it's coming - that train*
*To mutilate my dreams*
*To take away my soul - sing me a song -*
*stroke the strings —*
*beat the conga*
*Its coming - the train*
*Play the music - to move me - so that I can*
*move*
*Play the music, so I can dance*
*SO I DANCE TO SAVE MY LIFE*

I slept next to G.G. in the shelter. Mr. Valentin would cover me with the blankets that were donated by the church. He would whisper tales about strong African men in my ear as I fell asleep. When I woke up, he was there. "Let's go to the bathroom, my boy. We need to get cleaned up." I quickly jumped up and ran behind him. I like him. He took me for walks along the dirt road in Zachary, Louisiana. He took me to the church's basketball court and taught me to bounce the ball and shoot. He took me in his arms to hide me from the present reality. I was happy traveling with my family on this vacation.

*There's a place where the air smells of pine
and the silence sings pure jazz
To sit along the banks would be soul relaxing
I want to live there
Where living is simple, far away from the rat
race
Living is just that there
I want to go
Let down my hair
...and breathe*

I was successful this time. Man, I've been to that border three times already. The boss man told me to never come back to the shop. He wasn't paying me enough to feed a lab rat anyway. The customers knew I was the best mechanic in San Pedro Sula so those side jobs were easy to come by. There was no way to have customers come out to my house and besides all of the equipment I needed was at the shop. On the bus, as I traveled home to Límon, I could not control the impulse urges that poked at me. It's got to be better in the U.S. My brother lives there. Ronnie lives in New Orleans. Tio Papi Gordo sponsored Ronnie and my sister but my mama has six children. I guess he could only afford two. I always wanted to believe they would go back for me. But they never did. My girlfriend or baby's mama, as they say here, turned on me. She wants to be in the mainstream but that just doesn't matter to me. I'm a simple man. If in life I could work with my hands, have an occasional beer, and listen to Morgan Heritage blast through the speakers of my sound system I would have lived a fulfilled life. But of course, I wanted Marla to chase her dream. In fact, I encouraged her. She had my heart. Marla was a nursing student in Honduras. She wanted to be with a doctor or some other high positioned employee. I'm not the professional type. I'm a laborer – it's what I do. "Yo me voy a ir y mis hijos tambien." This is not the first time she has left but it is the last because I left too.

*Lovers…half remembered*
*Ghosts stalks sweet love's laugh*
*Wintry rain sweeps darkened twilight clouds*
*As teardrops slowly twist the past*
*Lovers…half forgotten*

Ronnie drove to San Antonio, Texas to pick me up. On the way, I told him how I'd hopped onto the cargo trains and witnessed others, who were headed US inbound be butchered as they fell onto the tracks throughout Guatemala. I told him how we, Christopher (my younger brother who had followed me this time) and I, were flagged in by the residents of Mexico and fed, and offered shelter overnight for a fee but because we didn't have money to pay or time to spend working off our debts we jumped from the second floor window as everyone slept. I told him how I slept in mud piles and drunk from grimy ponds from which wild animals bathe and relieved themselves. He told me he loved me and it was good to see me.

Ronnie introduced me to his wife back at the apartment in New Orleans. She was beautiful. Kimberly was tall with a slender build, mocha tinged complexion and a size 36D. She was exactly what Ronnie envisioned when we used to have heart to heart teenaged boy conversations. She was his fantasy because he said not only was she gorgeous but she is very intelligent. "Greetings, Valentin, Welcome" I just smiled and stuck my hand out to meet hers. The English language is not the easiest concept of communication for me. I understood her greetings but "Lord, don't let her say no more." "¿Como estes, cuñado?" "¿Tienes hambre?" she asked. "Que," I said. "¡Habla español!" "What," I said again. "Si, Kimberly, tengo hambre pero puede ir al baño, primero?" She directed me to the bathroom and headed for the kitchen to prepare a snack. This may not be so bad, I thought as I took a much needed water break. After washing up to eat, I suddenly started to think, "I need a job." I guess I'm mad crazy but I can't be without a job for more than a week. I need to do something.

On Saturday, one day after our arrival, Christopher went to New York by my sister. I met up with a couple of friends from back home that night. I was astounding to find so many Garifunas in New Orleans. I have also discovered the African history and culture held in this city. It made me aspire to learn more about my own history. I learned the Garifuna culture derived from Africans and Indians, Carib Native Americans, whose land was what we now call Honduras. Because of two sunken Spanish slave ships, Africans and Caribs co-habitated. They're language, food, and features among other aspects, were intertwined. "Buiti Guñoun," I spoke with Daniel in our native language. After telling him good night, I quickly explained that I needed a job. Daniel called a few contractors who paid cash money and …I go to work on Monday.

There are six people in the two bedroom apartment I decided to share with Daniel. But it's cool, we party. Paul is a DJ so the music blasts and the beer roll in continuously. I am having the time of my life. The United States couldn't be better so I thought. I got tired of that life, though. I wanted a family. I miss my sons! I need to make a better life for my boys. My wife is waiting for me but I cannot find the path to lead me to her. It sure wasn't Marla – I've been down that road. The right one is in my presence but only if I could close my eyes and when they open I'll be standing on that road with my queen at the end. I'll find her.

*A cerebral stroll we took across the Sub-*
*Saharan region*
*while I was spiritually dissected and*
*painstakingly placed together again*
*as one for a purpose*
*As I walked forward, each step meant I was*
*no longer the same*
*I was re-created for this purpose*
*I am, now, made from the gooey sap of*
*submission*
*and the fibers of virtue*
*HE has made my heart pure and able to*
*accept and distribute*
*My journey had for me, sweet soil that*
*nourished and cooled,*
*brisk mental breezes sent to sustain my*
*mental weariness*
*My journey had for me, a scene that was*
*familiar to my subconscious*
*My journey spoke with me and we discussed*
*that of which is my desire*
*I was taught to be found by you but…*
*Who are you because I am waiting…My*
*Father says wait*
*I have been fooled twice and joked once*
*waiting for you*
*Each time I thought my wait was to an end*
*but I lived a non-truth*
*My heart assures me that you are there*
*because HE has made me for you*
*but then…*
*I get confused and often burdened because I*
*long for you*
*I am slowly trailing confidence*

*and wondering if what my journey spoke was
true
I am outfitted to be loved by you...and still,
though outfitted,
I'm waiting too
I am ready and for you, I am looking to see
But My Father says wait
Because you have not found me*

On Friday nights since I've been here, we had been going to the same reggae club in New Orleans East. Crystal hung around my friends and me so much it just seemed right when she slept in my bed. She listened to reggae and spoke Spanish. We danced. I had no complaints. She was nice but I knew I didn't walk the path and she was not my queen. She was just there ready to go out to the club. It wasn't until I noticed her getting out of bed many nights, as we slumbered, to go out with her friends that I knew I had to move. We talked about it and disagreed and talked again. She didn't seem to hear me. Crystal was in her mid- twenties and living her life. Although, that is not very much younger than I am, I had to move. Movement is funny that way because I met Karasi at that club one night. She took my breath away. That shit was so fake to me to hear a man say those words. It happened to me! She danced on air, it seemed, and smiled bright like the sun. Her long deep black locked mane bounced on her head with every turn as it played peek-a-boo with me, hiding her dazzling dark skin which glowed like onyx jade. She smelled sweet like coconuts I cracked in Límon. I was intrigued by her mystic beauty. ¿Quien es esa mujer? ¿Ella es Africana?" This is what I asked the guy standing to my immediate left who was watching her too. To my surprise, he told me she was American and had a senseless boyfriend but he didn't know her well enough for an introduction. We stood even closer. I wanted to know her name and what made her happy. I needed to know her life's story. I wanted to hold her hand. I found that I was on the path and she was my queen, I didn't even know her. How can I meet this lady? I am struggling with commanding her language. How can I successfully communicate with her? And how do I get Crystal off of me?

She danced alone. I stood for several minutes watching for her companion to come. As I hoped there was none, I slowly moved even closer to her. I danced with her. Looking in her eyes, we danced all night. I forgot about anyone else being present. We just danced and smiled for hours. Crystal sat at the bar and watched me fall in love with this lady. 4:00 a.m. had quickly shown itself on the clock. Karasi said, "Good night" in a very soft whisper. I felt her breath on my ear because I bent over her stature. But I felt I could never bend over her character. It held too much without a word spoken by her. "What's you name," I asked as she walked away. "Karasi and what's yours?" We began to talk. I asked for her phone number but she questioned our ability to communicate with one another over the phone. I didn't care. I needed to speak with her again. Even if spangalish is what I had to speak. I wanted to see her again.

*Come... listen to my voice hum a sweet*
*melodic tune in your eardrum*
*As we soar together to a new sky that sparkles*
*a thousand lights,*
*twirl a thousand spheres and on air, we will*
*begin to dance, my friend*
*Follow me!*
*Come...take my hand*
*Place it along side your heart*
*and spark the trimmer that runs down my*
*spine*
*Let me feel the beat tell your time;*
*let me breathe your artsy essence as we sway,*
*Rising to the sky and fly with the songbirds*
*and hand in hand,*
*we will begin smile, my friend*
*Follow me!*
*Come...stroke the edge of my soul*
*Feel the surge as I pour my honey- become*
*your mysterious gypsy love*
*As I jingle the rings on my toes, snake my*
*globular hips,*
*wrap my searing wind around you*
*and spill out a liquid remedy for your reality*
*And, right at the core, we will begin to love*
*Follow me!*
*Come*

Six months later...

"Karasi, I don't think we have to leave! We'll be okay." "I'm coming over to your house and we'll talk about it." It was amazing how my English improved. There was a huge storm headed for New Orleans. Karasi said people were packing and boarding up windows. She said she and her children could not stay at her house in the Ninth Ward. "It floods around here when it's a regular rainy day." She said, "I'm leaving." I was frightened to hear these words from another woman but even still from a woman, who, I was convinced, was to be my wife. "Well, I'm leaving too – with you!"

When I arrived in New Orleans it felt as if I had entered the twilight zone. Everyone was moving about in a fast pace with petrified looks on there faces. Scores of people walked along the sidewalks or stood at the bus stops traveling to the nearest store to get goods. Bike riders carried sacks of supplies. Tons of cars filled the parking lots of Wal-Mart. People were stocking up on water, batteries, can goods and I was thinking about Karasi. "Does she have all of these things?" I had left work before receiving my check but I had one in my pocket from the previous week. This is serious! It makes me remember the place I stood when Hurricane Mitch hit Honduras. I held my new born son for dear life in hopes that we didn't slip down in the mud as we walked in the waist deep water. I fell down holding him. I thought for sure I had lost my baby. Marla held my other boy as everything floated into the ocean. Man, this is serious! I know this is not happening again.

I stopped at corner stores to cash my check before getting to Karasi's house. Either they wouldn't cash it or the store was closed and boarded up. She opened the door after I put one foot on the porch. This lady often scares me when she does these things. She said she's no voodoo priestess but she knows things - that's not normal. "Baby, I have a little money but I have this check that I can't cash." "Everything is closed!" "I have a few dollars, its okay," she said after she kissed me. "Do you still want to leave?" I wanted to know her plans and assist her with whatever she needed. "Yeah, but G.G. just came from the hospital and my mama is tripping." "I want to see what their going to do before I leave. Karasi called everybody in her phonebook warning them to leave the city. It was Saturday. Instead of being at City Park, this lady was sitting or pacing with a phone receiver to her ear. I'd never seen her like this. The volunteer evacuation became a mandatory one by night fall. The next morning I woke up to find Karasi packing and still on the phone. "Baby we gotta go," she said. Trey was walking behind her. That's my little man, Trey. He's a big, little dude. "Mommy, where we going?" It was 5:30 in the morning but Trey smells his mama, I think. All she would have to do is walk pass his room. He was walking behind her with a medium sized luggage bag, helping his mama. I stayed in the bed trying to make myself believe I wanted to leave the city.

Shreveport was a ride that exhausted me and I had just come from there. I jumped up with false energy because there was no changing this lady's mind. At about 8:00a.m., I heard her voice tremble as she spoke on the phone. I walked to the living room where she stood in the middle of the floor. She was talking to Ms. Amina. I can't touch that! Whenever she and her mother talk to each other I have learned to stay out of it. I remain quiet until they finish but what I didn't know is that they would never finish that conversation. I loaded her car with our clothes and cooler that filled the car to its storage capacity not knowing what event would come next. Where am I allowing this lady to take me; I have no legal identity in this country. Karasi drove to her mother's.

*Walking through a tunnel of darkness,*
*deafening sounds rush to the delicate ear*
*Step by extremely elongated step - one trembles*
*with fear*
*FLASH! then suddenly a radiant beam of light*
*crashes*
*unto the infirm eye,*
*folding up with excruciating pain, your head*
*feels as if it's moving rapidly in a gyrate motion*
*but there are no tears to cry*
*With blurred vision you think your coming to an*
*end,*
*as quickly as your feet move it's getting further*
*and further away*

*FASTER! the sound of pitter-patter moves as swift*
*as an arrow but still leaving you in dismay*
*The unrestrained pursuit of pleasure nags at you*
*as you enter darkness once again while*
*perceiving disillusion,*
*Don't be afraid,*
*It's only a way of life*
*Livin' in confusion*

# Bruce "Boogie" Carlisle

"Man, that girl is crazy!" She come in here early in the morning talkin' 'bout get up, please! We have to go." I turned over, me. "Bruce, what are you going to do?" "New Orleans has never had a category five hurricane and I know it won't be safe. I feel it." Is she serious? It's Sunday morning. "I'm tired – I ain't goin' nowhere." She talking 'bout what she feel. I told my mama sompum wrong with her. She ain't right. "Go head, Karasi. Leave me 'lone na." She walked to the back of the house by my mama. I heard her way up here. "I called you and you said you would be ready." "We going to the Superdome…" my mama said. That was it for me. I closed my eyes.

I grew up knowing my sister, who was eight years my elder, had some problems. She beat people up. That worked for me because at school I told everybody my sister was crazy and they better not mess with me. As I grew older, I started to understand her more and we became friends. I mean, we were brother and sister but she became my friend as I grew older. I knew she loved me but she never would say it. I thought because she didn't like my daddy, she didn't like me either. I started to resent my daddy for her but I never really understood why she had so much animosity toward him. I remember when we lived in Eastsho'. I was still in elementary school and Karasi had just graduated high school. She was trying to be an open hearted and kind person. I knew her well. She wanted to go to Baton Rouge for SU football game. Karasi had dance school that Saturday morning and after class she came back to start sweeping and vacuuming before my mama got home. My mama came back from making groceries later. Karasi asked her for permission to go to the game. Well, my mama was from the old school, pretty much. Karsai's boyfriend was in the band at Southern University in Baton Rouge, so my mama said "no." "You ain't going way," sung like a song, "to Baton Rouge to get pregnant!" All hell broke loose! Karasi went to screaming. "What do you think of me? I want to see the game; really I want to listen to the band because no one really watches the game. I want to go with my friends and yes, Edward will be there but he will be with his friends too. We don't get down like that anyway." My mama said, no again. Karasi went off! I have graduated from school, ya heard me, and if you don't trust me that's your problem – I'm going to the game." She started packing. My sister moved to Baton Rouge that fall. Edward and Shelley were enrolled in school that semester and they both had their own apartment. She called Edward to pick her up. He came all the way from Baton Rouge to get her. They were more brother and sister than boyfriend and girlfriend. Shelley shoulda been my sister too! Her and my sister was tight. You know they say when you mess up, an associate will be there to tell you about it but if the same situation jumped off, a true friend will be in that mess with you and be there to tell you how y'all made a mess of that one. Karasi and Shelley was always into something. Shelley was cool, man. She always had a smile on her face – Karasi too – which made me know they both were crazy. They could be pissed off and smiling, boy, I got outta their way. They wasn't like that much though. They laughed a lot, goofy that's what they were. I had two sisters, Karasi and Shelley. They were gone. My sister called home for me from time to time. I missed her so much that I ain't want to do nothin'. My mama told her that I wasn't doing well in school, if I even went, and it was her fault. My sister really didn't care that she said it was her fault but she always talked to me about school. She came home. She hugged me and said, "I love you and I will never leave you alone here." I knew she was directing that toward my daddy. But I didn't exactly know what she meant. Anyway, I was glad that she was home. We went back to our old selves, fussing and fighting but loving one another. When time came, my sister explained to me that she had to go away to college. She was going to Jackson State. She promised that she would call and I grew up without her in the same household, at that point, because even when she wasn't in school, she wasn't at the house with my mama and daddy. She lived with Shelley and her family pretty much since she was in junior high school. I felt her love anyway and I remembered the things she would say to me. I got into that Talib Kweli and Common; she told me 'bout these cats. I witnessed those situations, she warned me about. I knew how to handle them and move on.

Hmm he wondered
Wondered what you saw when you looked at
his shoes
They're not worn but brand new
Did you think he was the same guy you saw
on the news?
Or did you choose to case his outer surface?
Hmmm he wondered
Wondered what you felt when you backed up
a pace when he came near
Did you fear him? Or did you clear the path
so he could walk by?
Hmmm he wondered
but knew you judged his color which no other
man there shared
Slacks and coat, shirt and tie - white face, red
hair, blue eyes
Spewing out no discrimination lies
You judged his persona from your brain dead
stereotype
that earned your KKK stripes
Your granddaddy's daddy wish is what you
live by
but slavery days are no longer
Hmmm he wondered
and met your stare with a deportment that
was burly yet mellow
So you stuck your hand out, greeted him with
a smile and said "hello"

CORPORATE   AMERICA

Karasi came back to the front with bags in her hand. With her foot on my throat, she told me she needed me to open my trunk because our stuff won't fit in her car. "Wait a minute, I ain't going nowhere! Give me my damn keys!!" This is what I yelled as I stomped to the back to see what my mama was talking about. "We're going to ride out far enough to be away from the storm and come back," she said. So I grabbed my play station and Kenneth Coles – and woke Love up. Man, the wrath! After we hopped in the cars, we stopped over at my mother- in- law's house to see about the dog. Ya know, we left him some water and food, played with him for a while. By that time, Karasi was blowing her horn ridiculously while bumping that Mos Def. I came out joking, dancing to "I am the most beautiful Boogie Man, the most beautiful Boogie Man. Let me be your favorite nightmare. Close your eyes and I'll be right there." We were on the road. I was sleepy. Brotha had a hard night!

# Tia (Brumfield) Bostich

*Adhere to the lessons echoed from the graceful walls,*
*listen to the water muttered sacrificial calls,*
*feel the wind rush through to the bone,*
*humble your tone*
*as you enter the mystic silk cave*
*It is there, where, the first offering is held, it is there, where,*
*the truth is archived,*
*it is there, where, the future us...saved*
*She took me there - and we twirled around*
*the sun, the moon and the earth;*
*It was there, where, I witnessed the sea's breeze,*
*the flame of obliteration,*
*the drops of liquid requisite that worked as one for life*
*It was there, where, I smelled the spiritual bouquet held by Oshun,*
*It was there, where, I helped churn this black and red and green clay-like*
*stuff with Imhotep that later became a nation sharp as a knife*
*To cut through time, to slice the unwanted away,*
*to puncture all of the fearless kind,*
*to engrave a life sized print at the bay*

*It was there, in the cave, where, I started to
become confused
for inside of this diminutive casing were tall
trees and wide seas,
boisterous fires and plentiful leaves
which were replicating tall trees and wide
seas, boisterous fires
and plentiful leaves
It was there, in the cave, where, I started to
become confused
because they sang loudly and drummed
hysterically,
and looped each other in a million frenzies or
mo'
It was there, in the cave, where, I began to
glow
And frightened, I ran to her
And she stroked my little hand, and brushed
back my mahogany, thick,
coarse hair
Then she lifted me in her arms and extended
them to the heavens
and I grew and became ample and... cried
because it was there, that, I realized I was this
nation's first offering...
a small slave girl turned powerful woman...
I surrender
I surrender to the first offering*

My name is Tia Brumfield Sevory? Bostich?.
My biological father's last name is Sevory. I have
never seen him before in my life. I was told he

lives in Arizona. My Grammy told me he is from Mississippi. My mama, well, she answers my questions very matter of factly, oftentimes with one or two words. Sometimes I write those words down because I think if I put them together I will get a whole story that explains to me the reason sadness swaddles her face when I ask anything about my father. She said he cheated on her while she carried me. I put that together after three conversations. He cheated with his girlfriend before my mother. Eventually my mother learned of this deceit. My mother started to dress up for him and make sure the house was orderly. But he would pick fights with her accusing her of dressing pretty for someone else while he was away at work. He told her that she was fat and he wasn't buying any maternity clothes for her like it was some sort of punishment for talking back to him. She became very depressed after putting him out of her studio apartment. My mother said she cried and cried. My grammy said she acted as if she was dead. My Uncle Boogie said he overheard her tell my nanny Shelley she wished she was dead. Nanny Shelley came to our house everyday to make mama laugh. It was strange that it never worked at that time. My Nanny Shelley was funny! They were good friends – like sisters. My mother was hurting and my Nanny was too. When I was born I had two mothers. Although my mama called to Mr. Sevory in Arizona from the hospital, I never had a father. I had Mama and Nanny Shelley. My mama started coming around little by little but never, my uncle said, never like before. He knew something was still wrong. Just as I started to walk at nine months, my mother attempted to take her own life. She said life just wasn't for her and she was tired. Grammy said she was always a depressed child. She wore black and covered her bedroom windows to hide the day light after her daddy died. They said she was so emotional, moody emotional, as a teenager. As she sat on the floor, in the dark, with a razor in her hand and many others on the floor, I touched her, she said. She thought I was in my baby bed but I walked through the house, in the dark, and found her behind the dining room table at three o'clock a.m. and touched her. "You were sent to save my life." "You were giving to me, a gift to love, maybe you were sent by my daddy." This is what she told me as she wept one day. I know she was trying to tell me this story but I got it already, in fragments.

*Confusion tells me that I don't want to be in holy matrimony*
*because loneliness haunts my soul and unfaithfulness is in my spirit*
*Neglect shows me that I am not your first priority*
*neither am I your first pick of family*
*for your family consist of people far away*
*I cannot be them nor they me*
*Suffocated love tells me that I am dying –*

*I am no longer the same blossoming woman –*
*I am walking dead*
*I cannot breathe – I am not nourished – I*
*cannot be!*
*I have made the biggest mistake yet - times*
*two*
*For the next mistake came when the baby I*
*am carrying was conceived*
*with you*

*What a blessing to have possessed the ability*
*to bring forth life?*
*What pain to have acquired a numbed heart?*
*What am I to do about the curse of the*
*unhappy pot bellied wife?*
*What detriment to have a home falling apart?*

*As I take a step and render forth my hand*
*As I cover my mouth with hopes of savored*
*breath*
*I am not able to stand the backwoods and*
*wastelands*
*of the field that I am standing alone*
*Alone with a fertilized egg in my womb*
*and a susceptible baby at my side*
*Fighting the strong gusts of thick winds*
*while scooping her up in my wing*
*I am dying!*
*Rubbing my stomach filled with mixed*
*emotions*
*realizing the thomp I just felt was my unborn –*
*sworn to nurture by nature*
*I love this child*

*I don't see you but I hear the empty promises*
*of which comes from your*
*gut*
*Wearied I take another step, survival envelops*
*my energy given never*
*ceasing to try*
*but my daughter is watching me die*
*Loneliness hovers over my soul and*
*faithfulness is far gone from my*
*heart*
*Just as maturity has gone from you*
*as responsibility dangles at your outskirts*
*bouncing off as your sights are filled with*
*glitter*
*Can't you speak without lying about the un-*
*necessities you are buying*
*Can't you see your every word cracks the*
*essence of me – I am dying*
*I am dying,*
*I am dying, you are killing me with kindness*
*because reality you just don't know*
*I am not in your fantasy – I live amongst the*
*world flow*
*And I cannot live alone*
*As the man, my husband and this is your*
*home –*
*this is where responsibility lives and I cannot*
*live alone*
*Here is where I stop, on the side of the road,*
*choking,*
*with my child and my unborn, crying*
*In this smog filled existence, we are dying!*
*And we are alone*

Bostich was the name of my brother's father. He was my mother's husband once. But I watched her die inside over and over. I was so afraid she could be back to the place where she was once. She made a promise to me though. Because I was given to her to love, she said, a spiritual gift to remind her of the importance of life, she promised to never go back there. My mother, if giving her word, sticks to her word. She gave me her word. She carried me under her broken wings and stepped out on faith and her word. I still feel like she doesn't love me sometimes. She assures me that I am her baby, her first baby. She says sometimes her heart gets so overwhelmed that it makes her explode inwardly. I guess these are the times when she yells at me or pushes me away. She doesn't do dainty girl stuff but she tries. I guess I'll understand one day. But she says she's not a girl's mom but she loves me. I love her.

I never really say too much because my mama tells me to be quiet a lot. But on the morning we packed up and went by Grammy I didn't know what to say. My mama asked me again and again what was wrong. I had nothing to say – she said that was a first. I didn't know whether to be afraid or calm knowing she would take care of me. I knew G.G. was going to die because she had the same thing that killed my Nanny Shelley. I knew that Uncle Boogie wasn't going anywhere – it was too early. I, however, didn't know what my mama was going to do. She said everyone must go! She said it with her "I'm not playing, do what I say" look. I guess I was just quiet because I knew better than to say anything that may be the wrong thing to say. I was quiet until I had to go to a new school in Texas. I made new friends and rode a school bus. At home, there weren't any school busses to bring me to school and take me home after school was over. My new friends spoke Spanish. I was happy. It was almost like my old school where we learned everything in Spanish. They gave me uniforms and shoes. My mama said we didn't have those things anymore. My friends gave me everything I needed for school. They were nice. On Thursdays, at school, a production from a local church would visit. They preformed spiritual skits about everyday life and obstacles. The skits taught us how to overcome hardships from peer pressure, sharing, compromise – most of the things my mama talks about at home. I liked my new school. We even started going to the church. My family smiled again. That was until my mama received a phone call from the missing persons people. They asked her if she knew Tia Brumfield. It turned out that Mr. Sevory had reported me missing. I had never seen this man before in my life. He never called me on any of my eight birthdays. What the hell does he want?!!! That's what my mama asked the lady from Missing Persons. "Tell him my daughter is alright and she has been alright for the past eight years – And by the way, tell him she'll be nine years old, next month, and has never even heard his voice." "What does he want money, shit!

"Does he want FEMA money for a daughter he has never seen, except on a picture. Certainly he is not concerned, so what the hell does he want!" The voice on the receiving end was shocked. She paused and after my mama shouted "hello" she asked if she could report our whereabouts to him. Again, my mama shouted "No!" That was the end of that.

I can't wait to go back to Texas. I'ma ask my mama if I can go to my school and see my friends, especially Carla. Huh! We have to live in a hotel again in New Orleans. I don't know why we have to stay here. It is dirty and nothing is open. We can't go to the park to play because people are there living in trailers. We can't go to African dance class anymore because everybody is somewhere else. I hate this stupid school my mama is making me go to – the people are nice (except my teacher) but I miss my school in Texas. So I still don't say anything just like the morning we left this place.

## Amina Carlisle

"I'm not going no where." I remember Hurricane Betsy. My daddy went around getting people with his boat because water was at the roof tops. The levee had broken in the Ninth Ward, nothing can be worse than that. This will be just like the rest of the times when everyone got scared for nothing. My daughter seems to be loosing her mind. She thinks dooms day is coming. Every time the phone rings, Karasi is on the other end. "Get the hell off my phone, girl. Stop calling me!" It's so easy to hurt her feelings but she is persistent whether her feelings or hurt or not. "What are we going to do with G.G., Karasi?" Before I knew it, my baby was at my door coming to carry us away. "By any means necessary" she said. I'm shol glad she put up such a fuss. New Orleans was a mess when those levees broke. People's bodies were floating or being eaten by alligators. Lord, have mercy, my child got us out of there. I asked her before leaving, what are we going to do with G.G. but if we were still there, Jesus…

Karasi grew up as a troubled child. I thought it was due to the brain tumor. Most of her life, she has been telling me that I was wrong. She assured me that she is stronger than a label. She refused to be labeled by anyone, even me. I never really understood my child but I love her wholeheartedly. I thought she had no love for me at one point in her life. This storm has erased all doubt in my mind. Now I know Karasi would give her life for me and her babies. She carries the weight of the family on her shoulders. It's almost like she has the spirit of my daddy inside of her.

*Once upon a storybook love,*
*when daffodils swayed and humming birds sang,*
*a girl's warm heart was filled with the harmony of a symphony*
*When the stars glistened like diamonds and air smelled of natural perfume, she smiled*
*Once upon a storybook love*

*Once upon a twisted fairytale,*
*when shrieks of hatred soared through the streets*
*and trees bared "strange fruit"*
*that woman mourned truth*
*When bullets reign the air*
*and fire brightened the night, she cried*
*Once upon a twisted fairytale*
*Based on a true story*

Never in a million years would I have moved to Texas. I have found good in the midst of this terrible phenomenon. My husband is here and seems to be a better person. Lord knows we've had our battles. He takes care of me.

These days I have been so weary and forgetful. I don't know whether I'm coming or going. My daddy is gone. My sister is gone. My mama is gone. I feel alone at times. I never talked to Karasi about what was troubling me. She is my daughter not my friend, I thought. But I know a little better. My Karasi is grown now with babies of her own. She talks to me about subjects she has never shared, allowing me to engage in a healthy conversation with her woman to woman. I told her that I am scared. After the stroke, I am just not the same. I have no outward disabilities, all of my extremities are functioning, but my memory and focus are diminishing. When I listen to her tell me about my experience in the hospital (I don't remember any of it), it frightens me even more. Karasi's belief is, although I went through that dark passage way, it wasn't my time. She said I had unfinished business and God saved me for that reason. Since then, I was given a chance to dance at my daughter's 31$^{st}$ birthday party. I was given the opportunity to bid my daddy farewell after I had done all that was in my power to make him comfortable while he was in hospice. I have nursed my mother until her final sleep. I have gotten my thoughtful husband back, the man I married twenty something years ago. And he is getting on my damn nerves but I like it. I have visited a farm with animals I would have never been close to in my life. I am living and laughing – this is what Karasi meant. Katrina gave me the opportunity to smell the flowers and breathe.

*Yesterday I cried*
*Because my feet were dried and cracked*
*Because my eyes were weary and blackened*
*Because in my heart was a splintering pain for*
*my children*
*Because the fruit I bared for you withered and*
*died*
*I loved you as a mother of nature*
*and never before but…*
*Yesterday I cried*
*Because you stopped loving me*

## Embraced Dream

I dream of rivers
Ancient, muddy, stretched rivers
The Nile flowing near the temple of Isis
The Congo passing through Kinshasa
I dream of rivers
I dream of wading in the water by the
riverside in the ancient rivers

I dream of Solomon and Makeda
The bond formed between Ethiopians and
Israelites
I dream of the black beauty as Solomon lusted
for her
The son created by them and great nations
thereafter
I dream of Solomon and Makeda
I dream of sitting at the feet of Menelik

I lay my head upon a wooden pillow
and inhale the struggle of a Nubian Nation
as dirt pebbles burden my flesh
I dream of the Sahara when it wasn't a desert

Send me the pillow that you dream on
So that I can dream on it too

But can my dreams fit on your pillow?

I dream of Oshun
Of her lessons of vanity
Of her yellow and gold wardrobe
I dream of Xango

I dream of Kemit
And the black soil of today's Egypt
I dream of Nubia
The black man land
I physically slumber
and mentally live in olden times of the African
world

I sleep on the concrete faced up, arms
stretched wide
As my slobber drips into the mold and then
seeps onto the earth
And I hear the chants of the ancestors

Send me the pillow that you dream on
But can your pillow fit my dreams?

# Nobody loves a little black girl when she becomes a woman

Pampered and loved, guided and cherished, is the treatment of the little ebon princess, being taught right from wrong, heavenly from evil and catered to in the process

As she grows older and knowledge begins to expand and in society's eyes she's all grown up, no one can see the person within, yet there are still blessings filling her cup because no one knows what she feels inside, the only means of sanity she knows is to hide, to shy away from the world, to protect that helpless little girl that was loved and now all alone, from society withdrawn

She, who now feels into a corner she's backed so just like a panther she's ready to attack - anyone who comes near, she'll fear knowing they would somehow hurt her and bid her strife so to get near her you'll have to give her your life

No one loves a black little girl when she becomes a woman – like two negative forces that rebels against all men because they tend to abuse their own and worship other cultures crushing the pride and confidence they have within so she's never caring but approaching her you may but if she strikes at you with anger, remember you made her that way!

Society

## The Fault is Mine

For trusting, for talking, for giving them my
time
The fault is mine
For dividing my passions to accommodate
then combining distortion as one
For changing the moon to the sun, convincing
myself of thinking everything is fine
The fault is mine

## Dream Come True

I'm surrounded by white smoke such as
clouds
And I see ahead of me a man standing in a
bright gleam
With open arms reaching out to me proudly
And I, hoping to be drawn closer and closer
to him
But ... suddenly the lights are beginning to
appear dim

But still he's reaching and waiting,
patiently waiting with a flow'r - in his mouth
the stem
Finally we've met and petals fall
and the wind gently begins

## Call me when you're lonely

Happiness is oh! so hard to find and everyone
needs a friend
I'll be there for you, for eternity, for a lifetime,
till the end
Call me when you're lonely, don't roam, don't
go astray
Call me when you're lonely, we'll find a way
Call me when you're lonely, I'll be around
Call me when you're lonely, I'll never let you
down
I'll be there for you for eternity, for a lifetime,
till the end
Happiness is oh! so hard to find and everyone
needs a friend

# DEEP, DARK, CHOCOLATE CUP O' TEA

Steam fills the small romantic café
as jazz music caress my ear lobe along with a
romp pa domp
strong beat of his tender palms meeting the
drum
Mist on the top of my lip as I sipped my tea
and listened
watched him glide to the oval table topped
with a jarred candle
as I sat there with a quivering gut because
here comes my SECRET
secret because no one knows.......not even
him
He took a seat so near he tasted my feminine
soul
he felt my gentle invitation to intertwine
MY MIND WANDERED
as I wished I had a cup o' tea -
deep, dark, chocolate cup o' tea
"T" is sweet isn't he? the one who shares his
intimacy
some where's else
Isn't he taken by the attraction of another
sister
isn't he.........................Gorgeous
distance is my defense against my
overwhelmed passion,
against his smile
distance saves me...I have much respect for
my...sisters

There was a ring on my napkin from the
sweaty mug,
just as clammy as my skin is, as I attempted to
converse with this brother
and not gaze at him ( I think I did anyway)
As I studied his outward perfection
and weighed them with his outward
imperfection...
as I learned his soul...perfect!
Dark - and - Locked - and - Deep Eyes
Gorgeous
"Can I get you something?"
it was the waitress talking as he glided back
over to his drum
"Sister, can I get you anything?"
she said, as she turned to see where my gaze
led
" A deep, dark, chocolate cup o' tea"
I said a little above a whisper
"We have herbal, raspberry, green but no
chocolate"
very apologetic, she said
I replied, "It's okay I can't have him anyway"
I, then, walked to the door with my keys...
and left

## Unwillingly Devoted

Sometimes my conscious says stay away from
the touch that draws you near,
the words you love to hear, the smile you
adore so dearly...just attracts me
Sometimes my heart cries, "You'll be hurt by
lies, Don't be fooled by a love as high as the
sky," a feeling so lovely...just attracts me
Sometimes my soul yearns for a desire that
burns, his every sensitive spot wanting to learn,
stimuli forced so strongly...just attracts me
Even though I try, scream and cry not to fall
so quickly
Still...just attracts me
Sometimes skeptical thoughts roam the dark
paths and smother the touched base reality and
sometimes, though unwillingly, you attract me

## To My Faded Friend

Every time I see the street lights on Frenchmen and briefing leather on the table at PJ's I just can't shake the picture that flashes and

No matter how many times I wipe my eyes and keep a steppin' …

It doesn't matter because every time I see the water on the lake which relaxes me so and feel the cool whistling breeze and the leaves blowing on the trees I see the same picture that flashes and …

Every time I smell the fragrance of Kush I shake my head and rub my eyes and keep a steppin' but it doesn't matter because every time I see you…tasting my pubic juice flow

## He Makes Love to Me

*He makes love to me*
*with no physical touch*
*but in such a way my core covets*
*He takes me soaring high*
*I shudder as his voice launches vibrations to*
*my spine*
*I arch my back to his every oral caress*
*I rest my thighs and wrap my arms around*
*his cleverness*
*I open my heart*
*I open my essence*
*Open to his visions as he receives mine*
*Open to his dreams as we entwine our minds,*
*our spirits,*
*Our souls embrace*
*He makes love to me*
*note: this is spiritual not sexual*

## You in me

I'm diggin' you
like deep tombs hidden, holding pharaohs
Like the cacti spines in the sands blowing over
the Serengeti
I know you
like the orange flames that flicker through
candle wax
like the patterns on my palm
like electric currents when the switch is on
I taste you
Like coconut milk soaked Techini
**Like cooked praline sugar**
Like vinegar covered beets

I take a deep breath and exhale the sheer
essence of your spirit
I take a deep breath and sigh

You in me
Like the words that lived in Harlem during the
renaissance
Like the black skin I wear
Like
…damn
dried mucus balls in the nose
Like cheese in the toes
Like my tooth wearing taffy candy
Like loose satin panties
I'm diggin' you
…out!

## Erotica

Electrifying pulse, thumping moistly
Muscles flinching inside
Gyrating slowly without even knowing
but all these sensations working to hide
Licking the roof of the palate, tingling chills
rush through the bones
Touch me, please I'm begging to feel your
pulsating body, shit, I can't be alone
I don't even know your every desire but I
have yet to learn what controls your wilderness
to make you yearn
I don't even know how to hold your hand to
have you understand the inner me, to feel me, to
know what I want, to tease me, sort of speak,
ummm! almost like a taunt
To have me lose all focus on what's coming
next causing every sensory nerve to flex
To water from the mouth and the meeting of
the thighs
Stimulating, causing rolling of the eyes
Perspiration combining hot and sticky with an
open mind to everything,
not once being ticky
I have one question to ask as dainty as a sistah
can be –
Please just say you can do that for me?

## SELF-ESTEEM ISSUE

HE SAID, (WITH A CURIOUS TONE) "HELLO" TO A LONELY HEART

HE CARESSED A BLISTERING SORE NEVER SEEN EVEN WITH THE KEENEST SIGHT - THE FIGHT INSIDE BEGAN IT'S VOICE OF RESONANCE AS PROCEEDING WITH A CLOSER STEP TO HIS APPROACH WITH SKEPTICISM AS HE REACHED TO FONDLE THE DARK HE SAID, (WITH A CURIOUS TONE) "HELLO"

HE GAVE A NUMBER AND SAID,"WHEN YOU FEEL LIKE SOME OF ME, COME AND GET ME"

HE SAID,"HAVE YOU EVER THOUGHT ABOUT YOUR THIGH ON MINE" OR "MY BREATH ON YOUR EAR"

FEAR OF CLOSENESS STRUCK BUT QUICKLY ENDED IN DEFEAT BY COMFORT

HE SAID, "I LIKE YOUR LASHES" - UNDER THE GLASSES PASSES THROUGH THE BANKS - A FESTERING HOLE IN THE SOUL HE SAW - FELT AS HE MASSAGED AWAY THE PRESSURES OF LIFE

FOR THAT MOMENT RELEASING THE BLARING YELPS ALWAYS HEARD

FOR THAT MOMENT RELEASING THE VICIOUS ATTACKS SENT BY ONLY ONE WORD

HE SAID, "I LIKE YOUR BOSOM" AS HE HELD A WOUNDED SPIRIT IN A TIME OF TURMOIL HE AIRED A SOILED WOMB WITH HESITATED APPROVAL STUMBLING TOWARD WHAT FELT SO DAMN GOOD AND BRUSHING THE BARENESS AGAINST HIS BEARD HE SAID, "HOW LONG HAS IT BEEN?"

OUT OF A PUNCTURED HEART HE PULLED A HOOK AND WITH MY CURIOUS LOOK

HE SAID,

"GOODNIGHT"

## Perhaps with you

Complete happiness I would know perhaps…
Sometimes I drift to avoid dismay — I become
numb to emotion,
for I have come
to accept people for people
but with you perhaps…
I would smile in the depths
for that I have never known
…but perhaps with you
Imagine

## The Making Of…

Thuds of colored drops of rain plummeting
takes me to the place
where my ancestors lay.
They comfort me as they chant harmonious
knowledge
They play me like the woman, Dj*embe*
They tell me of my kind who shared my
dreams long ago,
who pre-molded my mind just as warm clay.
They sing… *haey ooh wee ahhh oh hay*
They pacify my wounds when happiness
culminates

The cool from the sweltering sun renews my
soul
when the dried asphalt at my feet tickle
Tickles, as my toes wiggle a dance of freedom
Shining from the imperceptible gold my father
bestow upon me,
I sing… *haey ooh wee ahhh oh hay*

My kin of yester reserves my soul
They settle in to the core
We sing…*haey ooh wee ahhh oh hay*

I am them

## Calling the Harvest to Refuge

Territorial Green Vultures...imagine
Straining the energy which adorns the heart
beat
tiny fraction of life-chiseled, rotted like meat,
sweet as kraut
clout hunters-X marks the spot but not the
punter of the ball
fall to the knees constant-ly be walked on the
side,
stride with no hip, smothered like a chop of
pork,
no yolk, just coke-cane to nourish the fetus
feed us no knowledge but trashy news -
media
needing a barrel with wheel to haul the steel
plated from the bull
full of contempt, anxiety
soulless wimp pimp the beauty that misplace
her royalty
loyalty to the poisoned filled cigar-rette, pipe,
syringe,
cringe at the thought of being pure
pour the boric acid on the brain
that sends shocks to the temple!
simple-minded, with scholar potential,
with maggot stenciled on the heart-apart from
the sense of feel
"Peel the mask"
My dream said in the night or the night said to
my daydream,

Or was it a dream?
So confused, abused by my own people as
they abuse themselves
Sells liquid bullets - sells powered attacks to
the heart - smart
But can't see, we can't see high
Drugged out on the program or hiding from
the real
Scared, ready to jump out and into skin paled
American embryo, been that way raised
Dislocated student, heard that way speak...
but just peak into the womb of Mother Africa
Climb
Launch unto the umbilical cord wet
Accept her amniotic knowledge, she's calling
her seeds- hear her
She's taking back her lost
but erect muscles spit at her as he enters
orgasmic disrespect
But pulsating climaxes squeezes her tongue
But the needle punctures her veins and fills
them with toxin
But the artificial, lubricating, chemical grease
destroys her hair
But the plastic pupils blinds her eyes
But the acrylic disfigures her fingers
As there on the horizon sits Mother Africa
She waits, she cries, she feels the slaps to her
cheeks
She knows some may never unveil
But yet, she waits and whispers in the night,
in my dream, to my people
"Peel the mask"

## Introducing Me

Truth is…
I am but what you see
There's not a special fiber that made me
I am but what I say
There's not a wicked utterance from my gut
I have but one face and my mouth is placed
not differently than yours
But difference shows my mouth stores the
words you hate to hear
You fear the truth, the very entity my soul
feeds to
True to my core, true to my ethos –
hunger for the knowledge of our intimates
I am the slime you stepped in when the
historia itch filled your being
I am the haze in your dream when you
grasped onto your Africana roots,
The vine you climb fleeing assimilation,
the very strings holding up your boots
I am the voice inside that whispers speak your
mind, feel your heart,
taste your vibes, smell the aroma of truth
because I am tired
Of brothas disrespecting sistahs that would
make the next sistah weary
to be one of you so she chooses blue eyes,
straight hair, bleach her skin
so fair but I am
In love with my people

I am like Dorothy and Toto circling in the
tornado and off to see the
wizard when I think of peace in this blizzard
we call life
I am Nena, Nena, speak Nena
I am great-granddaughters of the daughters of
Nubia
I am the one who vowed to be true to ya
Deus' divine creation, most sacred property
Truth is…that be

## May I Have A Word

As long as the world exists

To the prejudice white man,

Don't be upset with me because you can't be as fortunate as we who are of color, because you are not my brother. Don't be upset with me because you can't be as fortunate as we who stick together with our creed, because we all breathe the same air and accept each other as one and from your world of segregation we did not run. Don't be afraid of me because I am different and understanding you can't see. Don't be afraid or upset because God took time to color me.

From the depths,
A mighty race

## And The People Say…

Oh! It's in me
It moves up my thighs from my toes, I was
born with it
It moves through the air to my nose, I breathe
it
And it heartens my soul
Oh! What is this
I need another hit to satisfy this passion
growing thickset in me
What is this thing I'm trying to hide that
smolders through my skin
when the world's against me, or
loving me, or
shoving me down a road which I have been
before
But it externally warns and noiselessly teaches
the ones ahead of the
music, the dance, the food, the struggles to
enhance a people.
Man, this thing is in me and I stand swaying
Like trees bopping in the breeze and it tells
my story for centuries
It's humanities
It's poetry

"Up you mighty race, accomplish what you will" **Marcus Garvey**

There are times when our confidence fail and every unnecessary obstacle block our path. This is when we must move from the place that burdens us. We must create a vehicle to remove us from what hinders aspiration or physical gifts that we have worked so hard to receive. Some of us will work all of our lives for some physical attribute and just as hard work pays off, it's lost. This doesn't mean that dreams are lost. It doesn't mean life is lost. It only means that we must move and keep moving forward.

Never are we to give up!

Never are we to allow ourselves to be defeated!

We are beautiful beings created by God.

We are victorious!

We are strong!

We are precious in everything!

We are royalty!

God's people

Mayor Ray Nagin spoke to residents at a rally before the march held on April 1, 2006 in New Orleans. Residents and supporters across the nation marched over the GNO Bridge (The Greater New Orleans Bridge runs across the Mississippi River connecting the downtown business district of Orleans parish to Jefferson parish). This demonstration was to unite the masses in order to have one voice to speak out against discrimination, unfair elections and public education. Also, the march was to memorialize the would-be evacuees who were stranded for days in the flood waters after Hurricane Katrina. Although starving and soiled, they were turned back by armed deputies to their demise, seemingly.

The march, led by Rev. Jessie Jackson, was supported by such commendable leaders as Al Sharpton, Judge Mathis, Bill Cosby, John Legend and many other black political and social leaders. They were alongside leaders of New Orleans like William Jefferson, Cedric Richmond, Former Mayor Marc Morial and many, many, more. All mixed in with the residents (all races) of New Orleans and various cities for one cause.

# The Gumbo Bowl

It is April, the most beautiful spring month I've witnessed in New Orleans. The weather is breezy and sunny. It is just beautiful! I had begun planning an event that would soon change my life. I am planning a wedding. But preparing for a wedding does not bother me nearly as much as the hesitation to redevelop my beloved city in its entirety. G.G.'s heart would have been broken had she seen this mess. I am unable to sleep with worry of the possibility of a failed attempt to rebuild my home. I am unable to sleep with worry concerning the trickery I have to battle to save my grandparent's land. The true definition of the American Way is bare in the southern region of the country. The discrimination that lived dormant was washed up and exposed as Katrina saturated southern soil. Louisiana's state government seems to be pulling blind folds over the eyes of the city government. The Federal Government seems to be evading their responsibilities which are the levees. They are playing tug of war with the governor of Louisiana. The Corps of Engineers are asking for billions of dollars, in addition to the billions they have been given already, to secure the levees. There is corruption and chaos but the spirits of the people are genuine. People have gone back to grass root demonstrations such as marches to fight political attacks. Survivors who are stranded in other states are being swindled from their right to vote in a mayoral election this month, in the midst of existing confusion, because they are not in Louisiana. However, soldiers who are displaced in Iraq, under false allegations I might add, have the right to vote by satellite but not residents of New Orleans who are only out of their homes due to America's worst natural disaster. This city has been exposed for its racial biases that have long been a part its history. The media has run with a statement made by the black mayor of New Orleans; but they have swept away the racial statements made by a white political leader and candidate in the race for mayor. Pawpaw always told me to watch the story as it underlines what is not seen or heard. He said I should learn from the underlined story and tell it just as I see it. New Orleans was destroyed by broken levees not Hurricane Katrina. The levee at the Industrial Canal in the Lower Ninth Ward being blown purposely to salvage the French Quarter (tourism industry) is questionable to some but apparent to others. For those who continue to question the allegations, I ask: If the levee breach was due to a design failure in the year 2005, why wasn't that design corrected in 1965 after Hurricane Betsy flooded homes in that same area? I was told by older generations that the levee was blown then as well, for a reason that is unchanged. By the way, the President of the United States, in 1965, walked the streets of the Ninth Ward and personally delivered meals after Hurricane Betsy to residents who were in Washington Elementary

School located on St. Claude Avenue. He was there as the suffering began. The Federal Government left American citizens to die. It looks like genocide. The tourism industry has long awaited land that is owned by blacks. This city's history tells us this land proposed for cruise ship docks was the only land poor black New Orleanians were allowed to purchase. It is the lowest ground in the city but it became their homes. Pawpaw bought a lot on this land. He worked hard all of his life to maintain his property and the property of his neighbors. My grandparents are no longer with us. Their house has collapsed. It is completely off of its foundation and on top of my mother's car that was parked in the driveway. All of my family's memories were held in that house. We were their on holidays as a family. We were there to communicate as a family. We were there to love the whole family, in that house. My voice will be heard on the behalf of G.G. and Pawpaw. My voice will be heard along with the fight for homes in the Lower Ninth Ward community or how ever the land will be converted. My grandparents are owners of real estate property in the Lower Ninth Ward; or, they are owners of a fraction of the potential swamp land below the Industrial Canal. While the decision has yet to be made using flood maps that are issued by the Federal Government and electrical grids that are built by a company hired by the city, residents are without housing. Houses remain in a contaminated state. New Orleanians are not sure if they will be allowed to rebuild their homes. Bodies are still being found. Receiving trailers provided by FEMA for temporary living quarters are tedious tasks. After the trailers are placed on homeowner's property or in some community park, the lights are turned on after at least two months has passed!

Boogie, my brother, and his girlfriend now temporarily live in Houston, Texas. He has been searching for employment but his appearance screams New Orleans. Boogie is round; he calls it big sexy. His jeans are larger than they have to be and every outfit is accented with a bucket fitting cap with a brim. Not that he goes into business establishments desiring a job dressed this way, but the cap is in his hand when it's not on his head which isn't often. He is truly not a briefcase brother. Bruce drove trucks back home. He delivered liquor to grocery stores and wine cellars. He drove larger trucks before taken that job but never anything that would put him out of immediate contact with Love. Love worked in retail. The two things she loved most in life, besides Boogie, were stylish clothes and animals. They never heard a word about Fam, their dog. But there is a framed pictured of him in their new apartment. Needless to say, both their places of employment had been flooded and merchandise tarnished. They're working to start over again in Houston. Houston is where most of New Orleans has relocating. But there are many in places like Georgia, Florida, N. Carolina, Maryland and Arizona. My mother's brother was flown to

Michigan by rescue crews on the forth day subsequent to Hurricane Katrina without a way to return. He eventually received assistance from Red Cross and he, now, lives in Phoenix, Arizona. After losing his personal belongings and place of business, he is working to start over. There are some in places further away like Oregon, California and New York. Though, my mother, Amina and her husband, who is now a friend of mine, are in Addison, Texas. The healthcare system in New Orleans is very close to non-existing so she can not come home. In Texas, nonetheless, she is receiving the medical care she needs. We are grateful. Mama is working to start over. She has never been without Boogie or me, close by. She has never lived alone with her husband. She had never been to Texas and although, she doesn't particularly like it there, she is at peace.

I have encountered many obstacles in my life. The aftermath of Hurricane Katrina has proven to be the whammy. I believe survival is about movement. New Orleans is full of movers and shakers, which means the city will survive. I, and my family, will survive. I have no job because the independent African centered educational facility of which I taught Language Arts received over 50% flood damage. I have no home because the house in which I lived was filled to the ceiling with waters from the Mississippi River by way of the Industrial Canal. Even though it has gotten me out of harm's way and back, my little Cavalier is dying; so soon I will have no car. I am starting over and will succeed. Faith tells us no matter what's in our path, we have to make the next step. As an ordinary woman, born and raised in New Orleans and faced with personal barriers daily, that is how I have lived my life. This is what will carry us through. It doesn't occur to happen any other way. All is not well! There is major work to do! But I'd like to say to the world, we are not broken.

Nice try, Katrina!